DRUM AND BUGLE BANDS

Ruth Daly

BANDS

LET'S READ AV² BY WEIGL™ ADDED VALUE • AUDIO VISUAL

www.av2books.com

Published by AV² by Weigl
350 5th Avenue, 59th Floor New York, NY 10118
Website: www.av2books.com

Library of Congress Control Number: 2019938590

ISBN 978-1-7911-0594-5 (hardcover)
ISBN 978-1-7911-1396-4 (softcover)
ISBN 978-1-7911-1397-1 (multi-user eBook)
ISBN 978-1-7911-1398-8 (single-user eBook)

Printed in Guangzhou, China
1 2 3 4 5 6 7 8 9 0 23 22 21 20 19

062019
311018

Project Coordinator: Heather Kissock Designer: Terry Paulhus

Weigl acknowledges Getty Images, Alamy, and iStock as the primary image suppliers for this title.

CONTENTS

In this book, you will learn about

drum and bugle bands

what they are

where you can see them

and much more!

Drums beat.
Bugles blare.

Drum and bugle bands
are loud and fun.

EVANS

Drum and bugle bands tell people something interesting is happening. People come to watch the band go by.

Drums and bugles were used in the American Civil War. Bugles told the soldiers when to wake up each morning.

The Cadets Drum and Bugle Corps began about 90 years ago in New Jersey. It is one of the oldest bands in America.

The Cadets have won the title of world's best drum and bugle band **10 times**.

Band Hall
Stanbury
SYNERGY UNIFORMS
Dynasty
Festival
Disney
DSI
REMO
"The Commandant's Own"
YAMAHA

Drum and bugle bands play many kinds of music. Some music is from the past. Other songs are brand new.

Drums are important in a drum and bugle band. Band members march to the beat of the drums.

The **bass drum** is the **largest** drum in the band. It weighs about 35 pounds (15.9 kilograms).

VIC FIRTH
VIC FIRTH
sfz
sfz

VICTORY

The drum major marches at the front of the band. He tells people when the band is ready to play.

Drum and bugle bands march in parades. Sometimes, they take part in contests.

A **drum and bugle band** performs for **8 to 12 minutes** during a contest.

The largest Veterans Day Parade is in New York City. It is held on November 11 every year. Many high school drum and bugle bands take part.

See what you have learned about drum and bugle bands.

Which of these pictures does not show a drum and bugle band?

VIC FIRTH

www.TheBandHall.com
DSI
REMO

KEY WORDS

Research has shown that as much as 65 percent of all written material published in English is made up of 300 words. These 300 words cannot be taught using pictures or learned by sounding them out. They must be recognized by sight. This book contains 49 common sight words to help young readers improve their reading fluency and comprehension. This book also teaches young readers several important content words, such as proper nouns. These words are paired with pictures to aid in learning and improve understanding.

Page	Sight Words First Appearance
5	and, are
7	by, come, go, is, people, something, tell, the, to, watch
9	each, in, up, used, were, when
10	about, America, began, have, it, of, one, times, world, years
13	from, kinds, many, new, other, play, some, songs
14	a, important
17	at, he
18	for, part, sometimes, take, they
20	every, high, on, school

Page	Content Words First Appearance
4	bugles, drums
5	bands
9	American Civil War, morning, soldiers
10	Cadets Drum and Bugle Corps, New Jersey, title
13	music, past
14	beat, kilograms, members, pounds
17	drum major
18	contests, minutes, parades
20	New York City, November, Veterans Day Parade